THE OFFICIAL

ANGRY BIRDS™

SPACE

JOKE BOOK

HEE HEE!

HA HA!

HA HA!

D0063698

PINK TAG
TALIZE
BOOKS
Kids
A18705 5A

WHY WEREN'T THE BIRDS HUNGRY IN SPACE?
BECAUSE THEY'D HAD A BIG LAUNCH!

ANGRY BIRDS™ SPACE

JOKE BOOK

EGMONT
We bring stories to life

First published in Great Britain 2013 by Egmont UK Limited
The Yellow Building, 1 Nicholas Road, London W11 4AN

© 2009-2013 Rovio Entertainment Ltd.
Rovio, Angry Birds, Bad Piggies, Mighty Eagle and all related titles,
logos and characters are trademarks of Rovio Entertainment Ltd.
All rights reserved.

No portion of this book may be reproduced or transmitted in
any form or by any means without written permission from the
copyright holders.

ISBN 978 1 4052 6916 2
56732/1
Printed in Great Britain

SPACE MISSION: GO!

WHAT DO THE ANGRY BIRDS DO WHEN THEY GET REALLY ANGRY IN SPACE?
They blast off!

HOW DO THE ANGRY BIRDS ORGANISE A SPACE MISSION?
They planet.

WHAT DO YOU CALL A SPACESHIP THAT DRIPS WATER?
A crying saucer.

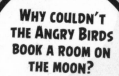

WHY COULDN'T THE ANGRY BIRDS BOOK A ROOM ON THE MOON?
Because it was full.

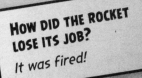

HOW DID THE ROCKET LOSE ITS JOB?

It was fired!

WHAT DO YOU CALL A PARROT THAT FLEW INTO A BLACK HOLE?

A polygon!

HOW DO THE ANGRY BIRDS PASS THE TIME ON THEIR JOURNEY TO SPACE?

They play Astronauts and Crosses!

EGGS-TRA TERRESTRIAL INVASION

WHAT DO YOU CALL AN ALIEN WITH THREE EYES?
An aliiien!

WHAT IS AN ALIEN'S FAVOURITE FOOD?
Martian-mallows!

WHY WAS THE ROBOT ANGRY?
Because somebody kept pushing his buttons!

WHAT'S E.T. SHORT FOR?

Because he's only got little legs.

WHY DID THE ROBOT GO TO THE GARAGE?

Because he had a screw loose!

DO ROBOTS HAVE SISTERS?

No, just tran-sistors!

TWO SATELLITES MET IN SPACE, FELL IN LOVE AND GOT MARRIED. THE CEREMONY WAS RUBBISH, BUT THE RECEPTION WAS BRILLIANT!

PIGGY STARDUST

WHAT IS THE PIGS' EXPLANATION FOR THE CREATION OF THE UNIVERSE?
The Pig Bang Theory!

HOW DO PIGS LAUNCH SPACE SHUTTLES?
By lighting the pig-nition!

WHAT DO YOU CALL A PIG'S MESSY SPACE SHIP?
A pig-sky!

WHAT DO YOU CALL A PIG IN A SPACESUIT?
An astro-snort!

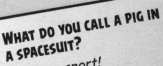

WHY DID THE PIG EAT THE SUN?
He wanted a light snack.

WHAT DID THE PIG THINK OF HIS LONG MISSION TO SPACE?
It was a bit of a boar.

DID YOU HEAR ABOUT THE PIG WHO TRIED TO START A ROCKET BUSINESS?
He couldn't get it off the ground.

WHAT IS A SPACE PIG'S FAVOURITE TV PROGRAMME ABOUT SPACE?
The Sty at Night!

WHO WAS THE FIRST PIG ON THE MOON?
Squeal Armstong.

PIGGY STARDUST 2

WHY DID THE PIGS PUT EXTRA SEATBELTS ON THEIR SPACE SHUTTLE?

For added sow-curity!

WHAT IS THE PIGS' NICKNAME FOR THEIR LUNAR BUGGY?

Their automo-squeal!

WHAT DID THE PIG SAY WHEN THE ROBOT GRABBED HIS BOTTOM?

This is the end of me!

WHAT DID THE PIGS DO IN THEIR SPACE SHUTTLE?

They all held hams for take-off.

SPACE MUNCH

HOW DID THE ASTRONAUT SERVE DRINKS?
In sunglasses!

WHAT DO THE ANGRY BIRDS EAT IN SPACE?
Mars Bars.

WHERE DO ASTRONAUTS KEEP THEIR LUNCH?
In their launch box!

HOW DO YOU KNOW WHEN THE MOON HAS HAD ENOUGH TO EAT?
When it's full.

WHERE DOES DR WHO BUY HIS CHEESE?
In a dalek-atessen.

FEATHERBRAINED FIREBALLS!

WHAT DO BIRDS FILL THEIR SPACE SHUTTLES WITH?

Rocket fowl!

WHY DID THE BIRDS LAND ON THE WRONG PLANET?

Because they were just winging it!

WHAT DID SUPER RED SAY TO THE ANGRY ROBOT?

Toucan play at this game!

WHAT DID THE ALIEN SAY TO THE ANGRY BIRDS?

You're all raven lunatics!

WHAT DID THE BIRD SAY WHEN IT FLEW OVER A MARTIAN DISCOUNT STORE?

Cheap cheap!

DID THE BIRDS LIKE VENUS?

Yes, they thought it was very pheasant.

HOW DID THE BIRDS DESCRIBE THEIR SMOOTH LANDING ON THE MOON?

Im-peck-able!

HOW LONG WILL THE BIRDS BE IN SPACE?

They are heron 'til Friday.

ASTRO-SNORT LARKS

WHAT DO YOU CALL A CRAZY SPACEMAN?

An astro-nut!

WHAT IS AN ASTRONAUT'S FAVOURITE KEY ON A KEYBOARD?

Space bar!

WHICH ASTRONAUT WEARS THE BIGGEST HELMET?

The one with the biggest head!

WHY DID THE BOY BECOME AN ASTRONAUT?

Because he was no earthly good.

WHAT DO YOU DO WHEN YOU SEE A SPACEMAN?

Park in it, dude!

WHY ARE ASTRONAUTS SUCCESSFUL PEOPLE?

Because they always go up in the world.

IF AN ATHLETE GETS ATHLETE'S FOOT, WHAT DOES AN ASTRONAUT GET?

Missile toe!

WHAT DO YOU CALL AN ASTRONAUT'S WATCH?

A lunar-tick.

WHY WOULDN'T SPACE BOMB MAKE A GOOD ASTRONAUT?

Because as soon as he started, he'd get fired!

ALIEN ANTICS

WHERE SHOULD A 500-POUND ALIEN GO?

On a diet!

WHY DON'T ALIENS CELEBRATE CHRISTMAS?

Because they don't like to give away their presence.

FIRST ALIEN: IS THERE A PLACE I CAN GET CLEAN?

Second alien: Just go straight ahead and you will see the meteor showers.

WHAT DID THE ALIEN SAY TO THE PETROL PUMP?

Don't you know it's rude to stick your finger in your ear when I'm talking to you?

HOW DOES AN ALIEN COUNT UP TO 25?

On its fingers!

WHAT'S LONG, SLIPPERY AND ALWAYS PHONES HOME WHEN HE GOES SIGHTSEEING?

E.T. – the extra tourist eel.

WHY DON'T ALIENS LIKE CROP CIRCLES?

Because they are so corny!

ROBOTIC RIB-TICKLERS

WHAT DID THE ROBOT SAY TO HIS TEAMMATE BEFORE A FOOTBALL MATCH?
Let's kick some ro-butt!

WHO IS TALL, DARK AND A GREAT DANCER?
Darth Raver!

HOW DO YOU SAY ROBOT BACKWARDS?
Robot backwards.

WHAT DO YOU CALL A ROBOT THAT ALWAYS TAKES THE LONG WAY ROUND?
R2 detour!

HOW DOES A ROBOT SHAVE?
With a laser blade!

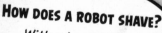

CRASH, BANG, SQUAWK!

WHAT KIND OF SADDLE DO YOU PUT ON A SPACE HORSE?

A saddle-ite!

WHY DID THE SPACE MINION PIGS BANG THEIR HEADS AGAINST THE WALL?

So they would see stars!

HOW DID THE BIRD IN A BROKEN ROCKET GET BACK TO EARTH?

With his sparrow-chute!

WHAT CARTOONS DO MARTIANS WATCH ON TV?

Lunar Tunes!

WHY DID THE PIG'S ROCKET CRASH LAND ON PLUTO?

Because he was only a ham-ateur pilot!

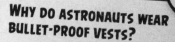

WHY DO ASTRONAUTS WEAR BULLET-PROOF VESTS?

To protect themselves from shooting stars!

SCIENCE SNORTS!

DID YOU HEAR THE ONE ABOUT THE SCIENTIST WHO WAS READING A BOOK ABOUT HELIUM?

He just couldn't put it down!

WHERE DOES BAD LIGHT END UP?

In prism.

WHAT DO YOU GET IF YOU CROSS A STUDENT AND AN ALIEN?

Something from another universe-ity!

WHY DID THE PIG SIT ON THE COMPUTER?

To keep an eye on the mouse!

HOW DO COMPUTERS MAKE JUMPERS?

On the inter-knit!

SNOUT-RAGEOUS SOLAR SIZZLERS

HOW CAN YOU MAKE YOUR MONEY GO FURTHEST?

Put your piggy bank in a rocket!

WHERE DO PIGS LOOK FOR STARS?

Up in the sty, of course.

WHAT DO YOU GET IF YOU CROSS SANTA CLAUS WITH A SPACE SHIP?

A U-F-Ho-Ho-Ho!

WHAT DID THE PIG ASTRONAUT SAY BEFORE HIS ROCKET LAUNCH?

Let's hope for swill weather.

WHY IS THE MOON BALD?
It has no air!

HOW DID THE BIRD MAKE CONTACT WITH HIS FRIENDS FROM SPACE?
By making a long-distance telephone caw.

WHY DO THE SPACE MINION PIGS SOMETIMES FLY THROUGH SPACE WITH THEIR EYES SHUT?
Because they know the universe inside snout.

HOW DO YOU GREET A TWO-HEADED ALIEN?
Hello, hello!

COSMIC ANIMAL CRACKERS

WHAT'S THE DIFFERENCE BETWEEN A PIG'S TAIL AND LAUNCHING A ROCKET AT 6AM?
Nothing, they're both twirly!

HOW DID THE COW JUMP OVER THE MOON?
It flew through udder space!

HOW DID THE BIRDS TELL EVERYONE ON EARTH THEY HAD LANDED ON MARS?
They sent a tweet!

WHY DID THE COW GO TO SPACE?
Because it wanted to visit the mooooooooon!

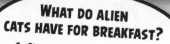

WHAT DO ALIEN CATS HAVE FOR BREAKFAST?
A flying saucer of milk.

HOW DID THE DOG STOP THE ROCKET CRASHING INTO THE SUN?
By pressing the paws button!

WHY DID THE COW GO TO OUTER SPACE?
To visit the Milky Way!

WHY DID THE DOG VISIT MARS?
To see if there was an alien pup-ulation!

TWEETING TICKLERS

WHAT ARE THE BIRDS PROTECTING IN SPACE?

Eggs-teroids!

WHAT DID THE FIRST BIRD TO LAND ON THE MOON SAY?

One small peck for birds, one giant cheep for birdkind.

WHY DID THE BIRDS GO UP TO SPACE TO SING?

So they could reach the high notes.

WHAT GAME DO THE ANGRY BIRDS PLAY IN SPACE?

Moon-opoly!.

HOW DOES AN ALIEN TRIM A BIRD'S FEATHERS?

Eclipse them!

WHAT DID THE ANGRY BIRD COOK IN SPACE?

An unidentified frying object!

HOW CAN YOU TELL IF AN ALIEN HAS USED YOUR TOOTHBRUSH?

It glows in the dark!

WHAT'S AN ALIEN'S NORMAL EYESIGHT?

20-20-20

HOW DOES AN ALIEN CONGRATULATE SOMEONE?

They give a high six.

WHY SHOULDN'T YOU INSULT AN ALIEN?

You might hurt its feelers.

WHY DO ASTRONAUTS LIKE TO DO SUBTRACTION?

They're always ready to countdown.

WHY DID THE ASTRONAUT PUT WHEELS ON HIS ROCKING CHAIR?

He wanted to rock 'n' roll!

IF ASTRONAUTS ARE SO SMART, WHY DO THEY COUNT BACKWARDS?

HOW DO ASTRONAUTS KEEP THEIR ROCKETS FREE FROM DUST?

They drive through the vacuum of outer space!

3
2
1
BLAST OFF!
HOW DID THE ASTRONAUT SAY SORRY TO HIS FRIEND?
He apollo-gised!
I WANT TO BE AN ASTRONAUT WHEN I GROW UP.
What high hopes you have!
WHAT HAPPENS TO ASTRONAUTS THAT MISBEHAVE?
They're grounded!

THE GREEDY PIGGIES' SPACE MOVIES

E.T. THE EGGSTRA-TERRESTRIAL

THE RETURN OF THE
BODY-SNACKERS

WALL-PEA

THE MEAT-RIX

MASH GORDON

MEN IN SNACK

THUNDERBIRDS ARE DOUGH!
INDEPENDENCE SUNDAE
THE RETURN OF THE JELLY
FLY ME TO THE PRUNE
EGGS MEN
SCONE WARS

STY ME TO THE MOON

WHAT KIND OF BULBS DID THE ANGRY BIRDS PLANT ON THE MOON?

Light bulbs!

WHY DO THE STARS COME OUT AT NIGHT?

They have nowhere else to go.

DID YOU HEAR THE ONE ABOUT THE TWO GREEN ALIENS AND THE SPACESHIP?

It was out of this world!

ALIEN INVASION!

WHY DO ALIENS TICKLE YOU BEFORE A MEAL?

They like a happy meal!

DID YOU HEAR ABOUT THE ALIEN THAT THREW AWAY HIS TRAINERS BECAUSE THEY WERE STICKING THEIR TONGUES OUT AT HIM?

WHAT ALIEN HAS EIGHT LEGS, TWO BOTTOMS, FIVE ARMS, TEN EYES, BLACK TEETH AND A SNOTTY NOSE?

An extremely ugly one!

DOUBLE CROSSING

WHAT DO YOU GET IF YOU CROSS A PIG WITH THE FIRST MAN ON THE MOON?

Neil Hamstring!

WHAT DO YOU GET IF YOU CROSS AN OWL WITH A TIME LORD?

Dr Hoo Woo!

CRASH, BANG, SQUAWK! 2

HOW DID THE NAUGHTY BIRD GET OUT OF SPACE PRISON?

He made a great egg-scape!

WHAT IS THE MOST DANGEROUS THING IN SPACE?

A shooting star!

HOW DO YOU CATCH A UNIQUE ALIEN?

Unique up on it!

WHAT SHOULD THE PIGS LOOK OUT FOR WHEN THEY VISIT STRANGE PLANETS?

Pig-pockets!

WHAT SHOULD YOU DO IF AN ALIEN SPACESHIP CRASHES INTO YOUR FRONT DOOR?

Run out through the back door!

WHY DID THE BIRD HAVE TO PAY A FINE?

It broke the law of gravity!

GRUB BUSTERS!

WHAT IS A PIG'S FAVOURITE KIND OF PARTY?
A cheese and swine party!

WHAT DID THE PIG EAT WITH HIS PASTA IN SPACE?
Dalek bread!

HOW DID THE ROBOT GET AN ELECTRIC SHOCK?
He stood on a bun and a currant ran up his leg!

MARTIAN MADNESS

WHAT HAPPENED TO THE FUNNY MARTIAN WHO ATE AN OXO CUBE?

He made a laughing stock out of himself!

WHAT IS ZOG THE MARTIAN'S MIDDLE NAME?

The.

WHAT DO YOU DO WITH A BLUE MARTIAN?

Try to cheer him up.

WHAT DO YOU CALL A FLEA WHO LIVES IN A MARTIAN'S EAR?

A space invader!

WHY ARE MARTIANS GREEN?

Because they forget to take their travel sickness pills!

DID YOU HEAR ABOUT THE SILLY MARTIAN WHO BOUGHT A SLEEPING BAG?

He spent two weeks trying to wake it up!

MORE MARTIAN MADNESS

DID YOU HEAR ABOUT THE MARTIAN WHO HAD A FACE LIKE A MILLION DOLLARS?
It was green and wrinkled!

WHY ARE MARTIANS SO GOOD AT WEEDING?
Because they have green fingers!

WHAT DO YOU GET IF YOU CROSS A MARTIAN WITH A COW?
Milkshakes that are out of this world!

WHERE DO MARTIANS PLAY FOOTBALL?
On Astro-turf!

COSMIC MISH-MASH!

WHY DID THE ANGRY BIRDS THROW THEIR CLOCK OUT OF THEIR SPACESHIP?

They wanted to see time fly.

WHY DID THE ROBOT CROSS THE ROAD?

It was programmed by the chicken!

WHY WOULDN'T THE PIG LET SATURN USE HIS BATH?

Because he'd leave a ring around it!

HOW MANY EARS DID THE SCI-FI FAN HAVE?

Three. A left ear, a right ear and a final front ear!

WHAT DID ONE COMET SAY TO ANOTHER?
Pleased to meteor.

WHAT ILLNESS DO RETIRED ASTRONAUT BIRDS GET?
Flew.

WHAT HAS A GREEN AND YELLOW STRIPED BODY, SIX HAIRY LEGS AND GREAT BIG EYES ON STALKS?

I don't know, Why?

ONE HAS JUST CRAWLED OUT OF YOUR SPACE SUIT!

INTERGALACTIC GROSS-OUT

WHY ARE ROTTEN TEETH LIKE OUTER SPACE?

They're full of black holes.

WHAT'S GREEN AND GOES ROUND AND ROUND AT 60 MPH?

A Martian in a blender!

WHAT'S GREEN AND COUGHS?

A Martian with a cold.

WHAT DO YOU GET IF YOU CROSS A MARTIAN'S NOSE WITH A GOLF COURSE?

A little green bogey.

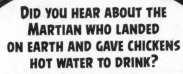

HOW MANY ASTRONAUTS DOES IT TAKE TO CHANGE A LIGHTBULB?

None! Astronauts aren't afraid of the dark!

WHAT HAPPENED TO THE ASTRONAUT WHO REACHED THE MOON IN FIVE MINUTES FLAT?

She got into the Guinness Book of Out-Of-This-World Records.

WHAT KIND OF CAR DOES A SCI-FI FAN DRIVE?

A toy-yoda.

IF A FLYING SAUCER IS A SPACECRAFT, WHAT IS A BROOMSTICK?

Witchcraft.

I WAS UP ALL NIGHT WONDERING WHERE THE SUN HAD GONE.

Then it dawned on me ...

WHY DID THE PLANET GET KICKED OUT OF SCHOOL?

It kept mooning at the class!

WHAT DID THE SPACE PIGS SAY WHEN THEY FOUND OUT SUPER RED HAD PUT CANDYFLOSS IN THE ENGINE OF THEIR SPACESHIP?

I think there's been some fowl play here!

EARTH IS CAW-LING!

WHAT DID THE BIRD SAY TO THE ALIEN BURGLAR ON EARTH?

Don't be robin anything from our planet!

TWO ALIENS WALKED INTO A GAMES ARCADE ON EARTH. "GOODNESS," SAID ONE, STARING AROUND IN AMAZEMENT. "PEOPLE HERE FEED THEIR PETS WITH METAL DISKS!"

WHAT DID THE BIRD SAY WHEN SHE GOT BACK FROM HER MISSION TO SPACE?

It's the best place I've feather been!

WHAT IS THE CENTRE OF GRAVITY?

The letter V.

DO YOU THINK EARTH MAKES FUN OF MARS FOR HAVING NO LIFE?

WHAT DID THE MOTHER ALIEN SAY TO THE CHILD ALIEN?
Where on Earth have you been?

WHILE LIVING ON EARTH MIGHT BE EXPENSIVE, AT LEAST YOU GET A FREE TRIP AROUND THE SUN EVERY YEAR!

WHO IS THE CLEVEREST PIG ON EARTH?
Swine-stein.

WHAT IS AT THE END OF THE WORLD?
The letter D.

SILLY SPACE TICKLERS

WHY DID THE ALIEN SLEEP UNDER THE LEAKING SPACESHIP?
He wanted to wake up oily!

WHY DID THE MARTIAN ORDER A DOUBLE BURGER?
He wanted a meteor meal!

MISSION TO LAND

THE ANGRY BIRDS HAVE LANDED BACK ON EARTH! THEIR MISSION TO FIND THE BEST JOKES IN THE UNIVERSE IS OVER. SO, WHAT DID THEY THINK OF LIFE IN SPACE?

"IT WAS QUITE A **BIRD-EN** TO MAKE IT THROUGH THE WORMHOLE SAFELY. I DON'T **WREN-COMMEND** IT FOR EVERYONE BUT **OWL** JUST SAY HOW **EGG-CITING** IT IS UP THERE!"

"SOW ... I'M NOT ONE TO HOG THE LIMELIGHT AND SHOWING OFF IS SNOUT MY STYLE. BUT I'D BE RIBBING YOU IF I SAID I DIDN'T SQUEAL WITH DELIGHT WHEN THE BIRDS FLEW BACK TO EARTH".
MISSION: COMPLETED

ANGRY BIRDS™

HOG ALL THE CHEEP LAUGHS WITH THE OFFICIAL ANGRY BIRDS SEASONS JOKE BOOK

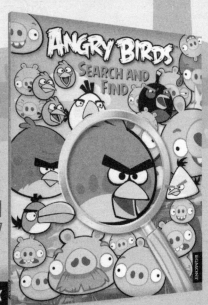

**SCOUT FOR SNOUTS &
SEEK SOME BEAKS IN
ANGRY BIRDS SEARCH
AND FIND!**

VISIT WWW.EGMONT.CO.UK

OUT NOW

ROVIO BOOKS © 2009-2013 Rovio Entertainment Ltd. Rovio and Angry Birds are trademarks of Rovio Entertainment Ltd. All rights reserved.